Fatherless

Fatherless

Fatherless

Annette Dunlap

Published by:

IPC

I.T.N.O.J. PUBLISHING CONSULTANTS
an L. McNeese Ministry

PO Box 2265
Clarksville, TN 37042
www.ipcbooks.org

Fatherless
Copyright © 2006

For information:
IPC
P.O. Box 2265
Clarksville, TN 37042

Take note that the name satan and related names are not capitalized.
We choose not to give him credit, even to the point of violating grammatical rules.

Cover Design by
Mr. Jonathan Snorten
J. Photography

Library of Congress Control Number:
2006907602

ISBN 9780976149057

- *Dedication* -

As I began to think of all of the people to whom I would like to express my appreciation for their support, prayers, guidance and hard work in making this book possible, the list continued to grow. I have therefore broken the list down into simple categories so that I could properly acknowledge everyone.

It's not possible to thank or even know all of those that support and pray for you when you are going through, so if I missed someone, please forgive me. God knows I love and appreciate you all!

First, to my heavenly father, the **Lord Jesus Christ**: You said in your word that you would never leave me nor forsake me. Life has been painful at times, but you have always been there for me. Thank you, Lord, I love you!

To my mother and father, **Raymond & Anita Fitzgerald**: Thank you for supporting me in everything I do. If God decided to make another jewel, it would be named Anita. Mom, you are the most precious person I know, and I love you very much. Daddy, I know you're not in the best of health, but I know your heart is here with me.

This book is also dedicated to my grandparents, my foundation, the late **District Elder W.W. & Evangelist Mary L. Harris, Deacon Ransom & Mary Jane Dunlap, Deacon Thomas & Mary Hannah**. Thank you for letting me be Annette. I will always love you!

Fatherless
<u>Contents</u>

- *Acknowledgements* -

To my son, **A'Darius**: words can't describe how much you mean to me. You are a wonderful, gifted, intelligent and handsome child. Never forget that you belong to God and so do your gifts and talents. We've had some rough times, but you hung in there with me. You knew when I needed a hug and when I needed to laugh. For this, I am forever grateful. Mommy Loves You!

To my sister, **Sonia**: thanks for ALWAYS being there. Even though you fuss at me, you're my girl. Thanks for having my back. I love you sissy!

To my PK sister, **Mary Sturdevant**: we've come a long way. I am so proud of you. Girl, I admire the way you just keep it real, Love Ya!

To my favorite niece and nephews **Latriya, Tim, Lil' William, Gene, Jamori, & El Jari**: Auntie loves you!

To my aunt **Fannie**: you taught me to be the best and to take pride in whatever I do. Thank you and I love you!

To my cousins, **Chetika** (Sweetpea) & **Bernetta** (Neecie): I think we're more like sisters. I love you.

To my best friend, **Isolene**: "Girl, we'll be here all day". I love you!

To my other best friends, **Shalawn Williams** & **Tonja Haywood**: I'm honored that God assigned us together. Thank you for walking with me, every step of the way. I love you both!

To **Glenda, Oscar** (OD), **Chea, Brianna** & **Charity**: I love you!

To my enemies, thank you. You all have helped to strengthen me also. I love you too.

- *Special Thanks* -

To my **former pastors**: Thank you. To my good friend **Calvin Reeves**: I can't forget your kindness in my struggle. Many others have testified of your godliness. You know the true meaning of Galatians 6:1. Thank you so much for your spirit of restoration and love. I love you in Jesus' name.

To my pastor, **Elder Jerrold B. Jackson**: Thank you for pushing me on my face, encouraging and praying for me to go forth in ministry. I appreciate you and love you with the love of the Lord.

To my daddy, **Bishop George T. Dunlap**, God used you to help make me what I am today. I love you.

Finally, to my publisher, **Dr. La Monte McNeese**: I know that our meeting was God ordained. You nurtured this project as if it were your own. Thanks for believing in me and helping me to get this message out to the masses.

- *Foreword* -

Imagine that you've got a deep yearning for the love, comfort and the protection of an earthly father, but he isn't around to provide you with fatherhood. So you turn to your spiritual leaders for counseling and guidance trying to fill a void that you feel in your heart only to be openly rebuked and rejected, suffering spiritual abuse at their hands. How would you react if the spiritual fathers that you were told to "obey", verbally abused you when you turned to them with your problems? This is only the beginning of the God-inspired testimony story set forth in this book. Many people fail to discern the true problems associated with growing up without the proper paternal influences in your life. Nowhere is this truer than in the African American churches of the United States where true and effective fatherhood is at a failing low. According to some experts, the reestablishment of fatherhood, as a vital social role in America, is the most urgent domestic challenge that we face. Not only are fatherless children twice as likely to drop out of school, but girls growing up without fathers are 164 percent more likely to become pregnant before marriage, 53 percent more likely to marry as teenagers, and 92 percent more likely to dissolve their own marriages. Fatherless girls are nine times more likely to suffer rape and sexual abuse (fathercare.org). A growing body of evidence establishes a high correlation between fatherlessness and violence among young men (especially violence against women). In the inspired words of author Annette Dunlap "this book is not intended to be nor is it a "woe is me", poor thing or a book of self pity". It is a true story that accentuates the splendiferous grace and charity employed by God to revive, reclaim, and restore one of his sheep. When for her, the path of righteousness became obscure; her life also became vexed with insalubrious spiritual and natural relationships. Just when one would expect God to step in, God did not step in, he didn't have to because He was very present every step of the way.

Fatherless is an intense journey that testifies to the truth of the words proclaimed by the psalmist: "Surely goodness and mercy shall follow me all the days of my life ..." This book defies the traditional theological restrictions often placed on God by "religious-minded" Christians seeking to encapsulate God in a denominational box. Some people love you because you are smart, helpful, beautiful or rich. Sometimes they admire your personality, your dimples, or the way you wear your hair. Some people are infatuated with your charms, others with your verbosity. Even parents have an emotional and psychological attachment to their children which results in love. God loves you also, but not because of you. God is not moved by the personal attributes that He gave you. He loves you simply because He chooses to. His love is self-generated, unmotivated, and never ending.

Fatherless is a story about love, not that we love God, but that God loves His children. His willingness to pursue them, chase them and never let them out of His sight is proof. *Fatherless* is clear evidence that if we take the wings of the morning, and dwell in the uttermost parts of the sea or hide in a smoky night club, even there shall His hand lead us, and His right hand shall hold us. Through her testimony, Minister Annette Dunlap teaches us that God is with us through life's special challenges, disappointments, hurts and pains, just as He is when we are experiencing life's good pleasures. Our health, our families, our friends and even our parents will at times fail us, but not God; with Him we are never fatherless.

Dr. L. McNeese

Chapter I

A Living Epistle

ᘓ *A Living Epistle* ᘔ

When I approached my publisher, Dr. McNeese, with the idea for *Fatherless,* he challenged me with seven piercing words: "What qualifies you to write a book?" It was a legitimate question. Authors of books are usually well-read or have done extensive research on a particular subject. Why did I think anyone would listen to me? I could draw from my ministerial experience, but I'm not even a pastor. Would my story be interesting or even scholarly? My education level was not comparable to a Ph.D. nor was I a foreign missionary. So how should I respond to the question of what enables me to author a book? The scripture teaches us that God will give us the words to say in tough hours and when I considered the question further, the Holy Ghost gave me exactly the right response.

From reading 2 Corinthians 3:2 it can be said that we are living epistles, known and read of all men. This scripture led me to conclude that not only was I qualified to write a book, I am a book, a living epistle! I may not have a Ph.D., but the circumstances of life have put me through a school (of hard knocks) that caused me to master in prayer and forgiveness. The Holy Ghost has been my instructor through a journey that must be shared with others.

Many fatherless children have not yet successfully pulled themselves through the struggles that God has seen me through. No, I'm not a foreign missionary, but I've been on a journey that has taught me how to suffer and how to heal, when to cry and how to laugh, when to pray and when to fight, how to encourage myself and how to lift up those who need a shoulder to cry on and a word.

Ralph Waldo Emerson once said:

To laugh often and much; to win the respect of intelligent people and the affection of children; to earn the appreciation of honest critics and endure the betrayal of false friends; to leave the world a bit better, whether by a healthy child, a garden patch or a redeemed social condition; to know even one life has breathed easier because you have lived. This is to have succeeded.

I wanted to share this quote with all of my readers, but especially with fathers. You need to know that there is no joy or achievement in life greater than raising a strong God-fearing son or daughter. Whether you are a father who has been absent from the life of your child, a mother feeling the pain of an absence, or a child missing the positive paternal influence that a biological father can bring, this book is for you. I pray that its contents will meet and achieve three purposes. The first is to cause fathers to repent, ask God for forgiveness and make a connection with their seed. The second is to help mothers to heal and to minister to their children in times of pain, and thirdly to the fatherless everywhere, I urge you to develop a love relationship with Jesus Christ like never before.

I found out that there is no love greater than the love of our God. He really is the best father a girl could ever have; in fact, with Him no one is really ever… fatherless.

Annette Dunlap

Nashville, TN - July 11, 2006

Chapter II

The Dad-Shaped Hole

๛*The Dad-Shaped Hole* ๛

There's an old saying that goes, *"Any man can be a father, but it takes someone special to be a dad."* I guess knowing the difference comes through experience, but for the greater part of my life knowing the constant protection and comfort of a father is something that I have longed for.

My parents married at a very early age and were divorced shortly after I was born. My father served in the military for years and later went into the ministry. Because of the demands of these two careers, I didn't get to see him as often as I wanted to. I talked to him from time to time and cherished the times that I got to visit with him, but it just didn't take the place of being at home with him.

According to Dr. Laura Schlessinger who holds a postdoctoral certification in marriage and family therapy from the University of Southern California (USC) and a license in marriage, family and child counseling from the state of

28

California, many adults do not understand that having parents split, living separate lives usually far away, even raising other children both bio- and step-, is damaging and devastating to children who "get to visit". "The pain I hear from children who feel abandoned – and therefore insignificant – has deeply hurt my heart". When I first read this I understood totally what she meant because for reasons known only to God and maybe some doctors, the absence of my father seemed to have a deeply devastating effect on my life. I wasn't exactly heartbroken, I just felt empty. It was as if the place in my heart that my dad was supposed to fill was hollow.

According to the dictionary, a father is a creator, founder, one who originates. A father takes responsibility, provides, protects and takes ownership of. For the longest time I felt as though I was robbed of it all. A few visits with him here and there were not enough for me. Sometime after the divorce my mother re-married. For reasons that I still don't know, I spent the early part of my life living with my grandmother, the late Mary Jane Dunlap. I really didn't get to know the man that would be my stepfather until my mother came to get me. My mother's name is Anita. It is funny, but I would call my mother, "Momma Nita", and my grandmother, "Momma". That's all I knew at the time. While living with my grandmother, "Momma Nita" would to come visit me often. I remember feeling that she was a very sweet person. She was always happy to see me. She would just laugh when I would call her "Momma Nita".

Growing up, there were two very important male figures in my life. They were my maternal and paternal grandfathers, the late District Elder W.W. Harris and Deacon Ransom Dunlap. They both loved me dearly and gave me the best they had, but there was still a "dad-shaped hole" in my heart.

I wanted my own dad, there were so many things that I had never experienced from my father. When I was 5 years old, I went to live with my mother. This is when I got a dose of my stepfather. I remember it like it was yesterday. I didn't like him. It had nothing to do with the divorce. I know that some children experience a vast number of emotions including hate and strong dislike when their parents divorce, but this was not the case. The reason I didn't like him was because he was mean, really mean in my opinion. I think my emotional state would have been quite different if I had liked my stepfather. I didn't like him from day one. In fact, at that point in my life I could say that he was the meanest person that I had ever met.

He was very domineering and controlling. At times I would hurt for my mother. He would say things that were so harsh, never a constructive word, just negative criticism day after day. He took rude to another level. Needless to say, I was not used to this at all. It was almost like a culture shock. When I went to live with my mother I expected things to be much better. Although we were in the same house, at times, it felt like she wasn't even there. I would ask her for something, and it was always, "ask your daddy." I didn't want to. First of all, I thought, "he's not my daddy". Second, "I don't like him" and third, "we don't have that kind of relationship". It is important for parents to understand that children often ask them for things in an effort to bond with them. Since my mother would send me to my stepfather against my will, I felt rejected and basically alone.

I longed, day after day, year after year for my daddy. I prayed and prayed. Of course at that age, I didn't understand the nature of divorce and all it entailed. When my daddy would come home to visit, I didn't have a care in the world. He just smiled because he was so happy to see me. When he left, the pain was incredible. At times it was as if the man I truly longed to bond with was so close, but yet so far away.

As a little girl, I couldn't understand why *my* daddy didn't want me. Did he not care? Why was I tossed to the side? The issue of having stepsisters and brothers was also very, very painful for me. My questions were, "how do you remarry, take care of, nurture, provide, protect other children and not be there for your own?" Oh, the pain was unbearable. I was troubled. I couldn't sleep at night. I later developed insomnia and fear surrounded me because I felt unprotected. I was so open and was battling with inner struggles that I had to keep to myself. When a father is not in his daughter's life, it opens the door for men to play on their emotions. We long for that male bonding, the covering and the sense of protection only a father can provide. Being a woman, I can only speak from a woman's point of view or better yet, my own experience.

My grandfather was a pastor and although I grew up in the church surrounded by lots of people, this had little bearing on the loneliness that I was feeling inside. People couldn't see what I was dealing with; their thinking was simple, "you're the pastor's granddaughter, you always get your way, you have everything". Well, I didn't have my daddy and that hurt. I think my grandfathers knew this. I was very close to them. I called the both of them daddy. The pastor, Granddaddy Harris would call me "daddy's girl." Granddaddy Dunlap had his own way of comforting me. He would look me in the eyes and tell me I was his daughter. Because I was the pastor's grand-daughter, I felt that I couldn't let my pain be seen. I learned how to hide my inner feelings because I didn't want to be an embarrassment to my grandfather or the church. Most people look at the pastor's family as being in the limelight. Church people have the same or greater expectations on us as they do the pastor. We are not allowed to be human and to have the struggles that others have, they act like we are supposed to be better disciplined, more attentive in church and almost perfect. Nothing could be further from the truth. To add to the problem and what's really crazy is that people actually envy us, if they only knew!

"There was a time when I suppressed my true feelings about fatherhood which led me to believe and accept the lie that I was not loved.
Today I have a very healthy and satisfying relationship with my biological father.
I love him, and I know he loves and values his relationship with me.
Thanks, daddy for being there for me and for giving me your blessings in writing this book.
I will always be your little girl."

- Annette

Chapter III

The Realities of Rejection

☙*The Realities of Rejection* ❧

A ll of my life it seems that I have had to carry some extent of emotional baggage. I know how Jacob must have felt in Genesis, Chapter 42:36

"And Jacob their father said unto them, Me have ye bereaved of my children: Joseph is not, and Simeon is not, and ye will take Benjamin away: all these things are against me."

When you are going through tough trials, you don't think clearly. It seems that everything that happens is specifically designed to hurt you. It seemed as if the devil had lined up a life of turmoil with my name on it. In the process of time my grandfathers passed. It was like they were just taken, snatched away from me, and that was against me. I had to watch as my father raised and nurtured other children, and that was against me. For the longest time I had no deep emotional bond with my mother, and that was against me. I was held to an uncomfortable

38

and unfair standard as a "pastor's kid", and that was against me. I was young, immature and worst of all had to watch as my own daddy kept picking up his step kids from here and there. "Being there" for them when they were sick, going with them to ball games, school functions or other special occasions, and that was against me. Little did I know, the pain had a name. It was called: Rejection. The seed had now been planted. It had deep roots and was now residing in me. Rejection is to refuse to recognize or acknowledge, to deny, disacknowledge, disclaim or to disown.

In psychology, rejection is an emotion felt by most humans when another person denies a personal request, particularly if it is an emotional advance. Repeated rejection (particularly of children) or fear of it, can lead to loneliness and depression.

Since I kept to myself, there was no way that I could have received any counseling for the feelings that I was harboring. I needed someone to minister to me, to give me a personal word, tailored to my situation, even if it wasn't what I wanted to hear, I needed it. Years and years later I was thumbing through Max Lucado's book entitled *"Mocha with Max",* when I came across these words which are from another writing entitled *"In the Grip of Grace."*

"God is for you. Your parents may have forgotten you, your teachers may have neglected you, your siblings may be ashamed of you; but within the reach of your prayers is the maker of the oceans, God!"

God is for you, not "maybe", not "has been", not "would be", but "God is". He is for you today, at this hour, at this minute. No need to wait in line or come back tomorrow. He is with you. He could not be closer than He is at this second. His loyalty won't increase if you are better nor lessen if you are worse. He is for you. Can your purpose be taken or your value be diminished? No, no one can defeat you. God is for you.

Unfortunately, I had no one to give me these words of encouragement. I often wonder if I would have made the choices that I made in life if I had been properly counseled and nurtured. It is hard to tell how the choices that we make early in our lives affect us as we age. Our current choices in people, environments, decisions, behaviors, and attitudes all seem to be connected to our early experiences.

One of the worst things that can happen to a child is to be left to themselves to try to deal with their problems. Like most people, I didn't like pain but there was an extra quality in me that always seemed to search for a remedy for any type of discomfort.

A quick fix or long term solution, it didn't matter to me, there was a hole in my heart, and I had to fill it with something. As I grew older, I took control of my own life and started making decisions for my immediate future. I decided that I would leave the church when I turned 18. At the age of 13, I smoked for the first time. Although it was just a cigarette, it made me feel dizzy all day. It took some time, but I finally got the hang of it. I began to like smoking, it made me feel cool. After a while, I began to love it, but it wasn't enough. About two years later I smoked my first joint. I was so high that at first I didn't even know that I was high. I just laughed, everything was funny. Ever since I was

7 years old, I had been in church, singing, praying, clapping and speaking in tongues and suddenly I found my spiritual condition spiraling downwards fast. Soon I had my first drink; it was called "Mad Dog". I remember it because I was a cheerleader and we had a game that night and it was one of the best times that I had ever had outside of church because there was no pain. I felt so good; NO PAIN. I still went to church, but I was trying to live both lives. I wanted to be saved, but I needed more than I was getting from the pews. I felt the way the Apostle Paul described it in Romans, chapter 7:

*"I don't understand myself at all, for I really want to do what is right, but I don't do it. Instead, I do the very thing I hate.
I know perfectly well that what I am doing is wrong, and my bad conscience shows that I agree that the law is good.*

But I can't help myself, because it is sin inside me that makes me do these evil things. I know I am rotten through and through so far as my old sinful nature is concerned. No matter which way I turn, I can't make myself do right. I want to, but I can't. When I want to do good, I don't. And when I try not to do wrong, I do it anyway. But if I am doing what I don't want to do, I am not really the one doing it; the sin within me is doing it. It seems to be a fact of life that when I want to do what is right, I inevitably do what is wrong. I love God's law with all my heart. But there is another law at work within me that is at war with my mind. This law wins the fight and makes me a slave to the sin that is still within me. Oh, what a miserable person I am! Who will free me from this life that is dominated by sin?"

Romans 7:15-24, New Living Translation

When I was 15 years old, I had an affair with a married man. For the purpose of this book, "Terrell" was his name. I had known him for a while and believe it or not, at first, I didn't like him at all. He was always trying to be somebody's hero, always coming to the rescue. I tried to ignore him and I told myself that he was just nosy. As time went on and I continued to struggle with my life and identity, there he was, *Mr. Rescue*. I began talking to him about my problems. At the time, he was going through some issues too. So we became close and leaned on each other. Hindsight enables me to ask myself questions that I was not able to ask back in the day. I now see that it is never a good idea for two needy people to lean on each other for emotional support. I now see clearly that I should have respected his family, his career, his wife. But after all that I was dealing with and the fact that I was a mere child when it began, which of us should have been the strongest? How could I have helped him or anyone else with their problems since I had emotional issues of my own? Since he was much older than me, shouldn't he have known better? Shouldn't he have been the one to prevent our illicit affair? Well, as the old adage goes, "you can't unscramble an egg". We would talk every day and then it happened, our first kiss. I'll never forget it. Then, we finally made love. As I said earlier, he was quite a bit older than I, so he knew what to do. I didn't. I was a virgin. As time went on, I grew deeper and deeper in love with him. I wanted him all to myself, but he was married. I never had the heart to ask him to leave her because they had children, and besides, he would never let another man raise his kids. And trust me, as bad as it hurt, I understood that. At the age of 18 I became pregnant by him. It almost scared the life out of me. I'm a pew baby; I grew up in church, on the way to church or getting ready for church. I was not very street smart and I didn't know what to do, so I confided in my cousin. Unfortunately for me, the news troubled her so badly that she told her husband and that very same night, we all ended up at my grandfather's house. Being the pastor of the church I would assume that my granddaddy was very embarrassed. One thing I didn't have to guess about was his anger. He was so mad, basically because the man that I had the affair with was a minister. My grandparents saw that he and I were getting close and tried to warn us, but it was to no avail. I think we were all scared half to death because everybody knew my granddaddy didn't play. I was so naïve; I remember thinking that I wanted to make the whole thing right, so I decided to do what I thought the Bible said. I waited a while and then went to apologize to his wife, another very bad idea, at least at the time. She was furious and said she would never forgive me. So, I left broken and confused. Anyone that has been through a mentally painful abortion or lost a child can tell you that satan will attack you with all that he has in his arsenal once he thinks he has something that really works against you. I told the Lord that I wanted to expose the devil and his tactics in every way I can which leads me to the next very important part of my testimony on his wiles and weapons.

"And I will restore to you the years that the locust hath eaten, the cankerworm, and the caterpillar, and the palmerworm, my great army which I sent among you. And ye shall eat plenty, and be satisfied, and praise the name of the Lord your God, that hath dealt wondrously with you: and my people shall never be ashamed."

Joel 2:25-26

<u>*Chapter IV*</u>

I Processed it the Wrong Way

CRI Processed it The Wrong Way SO

You can call it what you want, but it felt like mockery. There are some things that can happen to you that affect you mentally and emotionally, causing you to process things differently than other people. My relationship, or lack thereof, with my earthly father impacted every area of my life. The way a father raises you, or doesn't raise you, can result in hurt and feelings of anger. Those feelings can also lead to many problems and even make you feel far away from God. One of the worst results is when we set out looking for human love which is never enough to satisfy our hearts let alone our hurts. We need something to heal the wounds that we collect as we grow up especially if we are forced to grow up fatherless. Things that normally go unnoticed by most people can be monumental to a fatherless child. My interaction with my father and his "other" kids, (stepchildren) was very trying. For example, when I heard my stepsisters and brothers call him, "Daddy", my interpretation of that was mockery.

To me, they were laughing and saying, "In your face". For the life of me, I just didn't understand. That was my song, "I don't understand". Even after over 40 years of thinking, praying and raising a son as a single parent, I still don't understand. I can't even image being separated from my child. Of course, this is a mother and possibly even indignation talking. During my trials I was often reminded that the word of the Lord says that He will not put more on us than we can bear. I told the Lord, "OK, if you say so." God could have very well placed us in what we would call the perfect family structure. But He already knew the pattern (plan) for our lives. The trials that we are put in are to help shape and strengthen us. Tests and trials are to mold us and mature us. They are to give us character. For years I had a victim mentality. Everything was an attack. If I had an idea and it was rejected, I would take it personally. I was once told by a leader, that if you are not liked in an environment and you have an idea, you have to pretend that the idea came from someone else so that it would be accepted. As well meaning as he was, this was simply bad advice which helped me only to believe that it wasn't the idea that was being rejected, it was me. Thanks be to

God who will not allow more to come upon us than we are able to bear.

When people (mainly the saints) would try to push me to the back or to degrade me with personal attacks, somehow God would bring me to the front. Not to be undone, the flesh, and the devil remained busy, keeping me from seeing God. Many times I saw only the attack. It appeared that I was always in the second position. For instance, when it came to my father, I was after his immediate family. I hid as a background singer for years, because I didn't feel that I was good enough for the lead. It is like being in the choir, if you don't do a lot of thrills, runs or have a high vocal range, you don't get the lead part. In relationships, it seemed that I was always second to the main girl. I was the chick on the side. That's how it seemed, that's how I felt, and that was my position. So, I sought love that way. Having fallen into adultery for years and bearing the TOTAL burden for that, it appears even now that thanks to an ungodly spiritual board of judges, the man that committed the sin with me got off scot-free. He appears at times to be living a prosperous life. I can totally relate to the woman in the Bible who was caught in adultery. I lived it. If I called someone, and they didn't answer or didn't return my call, I took it as a personal attack. I know that sounds crazy, but the devil will always blind you to the truth if he can. At this stage of my life, I really couldn't see it any other way.

On my 40th birthday, I wanted my family to give me a birthday party. It ended up with me planning everything. My sister got the banner and balloons. There was hardly anybody there. One of my relatives came in, she and her significant other, and he said, "Man, there's not a lot of people here. I guess nobody loves you." That cut me like a knife. In my heart, I felt that he was right. What's the use, but something in me fought back and made me say: "God loves me." Did I believe it? No, but it sounded good at the time. I even had to pay for my own meal. What's even funnier is that the love that the world was giving me, I wanted from my family and the saints. The people that I was supposed to be ministering to, they ministered to me. Boy, they did it up big, but somehow I knew that was a trick of the enemy. It's like the devil was saying: "I'll love you the way you want. I'll give you all of that and then some." I couldn't go out like that. Even though I didn't believe God loved me, I held on to it anyway. Even when it came to my grandmother, the late Evangelist Mary L. Harris, I felt like she was always putting me down. It seemed like nothing I did, was ever good enough for her. Little did I know that she was nurturing me for the ministry. In my state of mind I couldn't see that. I thought that she was trying to make me like her. We would argue about it all the time. I didn't know that while I was helping her with her book of poems, that I would be writing this book today. I didn't know that she would make me study my Sunday school lesson because she was preparing me for teaching. She just got on my nerves with that. Before her demise, she sat me down and had a long talk with me. She told me that she has given me all that she had. She said: "Do something with it. You have everything you need." At first I felt 2 feet tall, but she began to tell me about some things in her life and we got closer than ever before, then she died. I went into a state of depression for about 5-6 years, just being depressed. I would sleep all the time because I just wanted the days to hurry up and go so I could die. I wanted this to be over. Then, I learned to live with it. I functioned in depression. I would never show it in front of my son, but I didn't have to fake it behind closed doors. If I was home, I was always in a dark room with all the shades down. Everything had to be dark, even my clothes. I wore black religiously. I went to a praise meeting one night. I was a singer and a minister of music. The group that I was singing with at that time had to sing at the meeting. At the altar call, the minister called me out. I had learned to function so well in a depressed state that I had forgotten that I was in depression. It had become a way of life. He told me that I was in a state of depression and that I didn't

52

know it. He said that he could see me at home in a dark house with the shades pulled down, not opening the door. No sunlight. He said: "I bet you have a closet full of black don't you?" I said: "Yes". He was right. I had a friend that would come over and open the doors, and pull up the shades, and make all kinds of noise. She would give me a headache. Actually, she was trying to help me to see the light. If you ever feel insignificant, unimportant or inferior living with feelings of rejection, self-consciousness or feeling that people are always judging you, you have to remember that even if your earthly mother or father leave, fail or reject you, your heavenly father will never leave you or forsake you. If you feel that there may be pain in your heart from processing things the wrong way or from the way you were raised, trust God. You will soon find satisfaction and healing in your life knowing that God is your father forever!

"Rejection is a killer. It doesn't come to just hurt you -

It wants to kill you."

Annette Dunlap

<u>*Chapter V*</u>

satan's Wiles and Weapons of Death

C&satan's Wiles and Weapons Of Death&

First, for the record, let me make one thing very clear. I think the scripture says it best in Isaiah 54:17 (KJV).

No weapon that is formed against thee shall prosper; and every tongue that shall rise against thee in judgment thou shalt condemn. This is the heritage of the servants of the LORD, and their righteousness is of me, saith the LORD.

When you see people who are always hurt, angry, mean, negative, feeling victimized, pessimistic and sarcastic, you can be sure that the enemy has deposited some parts of the weapons of death in them. You can see the impact in their lives and hearts when they're filled with the works of the flesh, to include, hatred, murder, envy, jealousy, variance, evil desires and the thoughts that bring on those desires. We see it when they boast and strive to be superior over others because they feel inferior in their soul and ironically many of these traits are seen among people that God has at one time delivered from the world. When you give your life to Jesus, hell releases demons to fight you. They don't want to simply hurt you, they want to kill you. First, they want to kill your joy and enthusiasm. They know that if they can get to you spiritually and mentally, they can make you self-destruct physically.

I think that it is important to explain what I mean by the title, *"Weapons of Death"*. The Apostle Paul once said that he had a thorn in the flesh. He called it, "the Messenger of satan" it was Paul's opinion that this pain or trouble that he was having was designed to keep him humble. Notice how the passage reads:

2 Corinthians 12:7- 10

[7] *"And lest I should be exalted above measure through the abundance of the revelations, there was given to me a thorn in the flesh, the messenger of satan to buffet me, lest I should be exalted above measure.*
[8] *For this thing I besought the Lord thrice, that it might depart from me.*
[9] *And he said unto me, My grace is sufficient for thee: for my strength is made perfect in weakness. Most gladly therefore will I rather glory in my infirmities, that the power of Christ may rest upon me.*

[10] Therefore I take pleasure in infirmities, in reproaches, in necessities, in persecutions, in distresses for Christ's sake: for when I am weak, then am I strong."

People have guessed and wondered for years at what Paul was talking about. What was his infirmity, was it an infirmity? What exactly was this thing that came to buffet him? The word "buffet" means:

1.   To hit or beat, especially repeatedly

2.   To strike against forcefully; batter or to beat

3.   To drive or force with or as if with repeated blows

4.   To force (one's way) with difficulty.

Paul knew exactly what God was allowing to be the thorn in his flesh. He said it was designed to keep him humble. Sometimes we can figure out why we go through things and at other times we just have to endure them and trust God. Like Paul, I know exactly what was buffeting me. He called them messengers of satan, but for me they were, "Weapons of Death". I admit that this title, "Weapons of Death" was chosen several years ago and probably chosen by me in one of my negative moments when I was feeling like I had been attacked. I chose to keep this title because it best reflects my testimony and it gives me a sweeter victory when I consider that satan tried, but he couldn't kill me. In his failure, these were the weapons of death that were assigned to me:

Rejection: This began as a child. I felt rejected by my biological father and later rejected by the man that I (unlawfully) fell in love with. My cry for forgiveness was rejected by men of God, whom I trusted. One of the devil's biggest tricks is to get us on bad terms with our spiritual families. When the heads of the spiritual house reject you, you can expect the rest of the body to follow suit.

Un-forgiveness: This spirit showed its ugly head when I tried to reach out for forgiveness and was laughed at and called names both by my spiritual fathers as well as those that I had hurt. I also withdrew and rejected (for a while) the love that God was trying to bestow upon me in bringing me back.

Lies: You know the old saying, "if you tell one lie you will have to tell another". All sin is based on lies, but when you are trying to live for God and trying to come back, lies can be devastating. People lied on me and the devil used it to his advantage.

Man pleasing – Sex: The enemy used a 28 year old preacher to entice me and take advantage of my 15 year old emotional status. Youth and lust are common partners and although sex is of God and created by God, like fire, it can easily be misused and can drive you crazy. Many people engage in sex in their attempt to deal with much deeper issues. In the process sex, especially through fornication and adultery, can place heavy emotional demands and place us in physical dangers that are just too much for us to handle. But what else can a young girl do to make a man (or boy) like her when she is trying to feel loved? Should she consult her spiritual fathers for advice?

Insecurity: This is almost synonymous with feeling alone. Who would protect me from the big bad wolves of the world? My daddy was not there, the ministers proved to have had issues of their own. What could give me the courage to face the world and my problems? I didn't know, but the devil did. Through insecurity he introduced me to many methods of gaining false courage. I guarded my heart and life by hiding behind drugs, especially acid. It made me think that I was the person that satan did not want me to be.

Deceit: Sin is founded in deception. First it is interesting, then it gets exciting, then it gets pleasing, then it gets easy then it gets habitual, then it becomes destructive. You learn to defend your sin with lies, but not until you have begun thinking that you are okay. Deception is bad, but self-deception is the most lethal.

Self-pity: Self-pity if not dealt with, can almost always lead to suicide.

Anger: "Be ye angry and sin not ..." is what we are taught by scripture (Ephesians 4:26). Anger can lead to positive changes in one's life or circumstance, but when it is allowed to bake, it creates a powder keg situation that leads to hatred and even revenge.

Bitterness: This is probably the most hidden of the weapons of death because it lingers even after you have supposedly forgiven others. It takes either a trained psychologist or the anointing of the Holy Ghost to discern bitterness. Only God can cleanse us properly from this terrible deep seated personality flaw. If bitterness is left unchallenged, it can lead to all types of physical illnesses as well as the banishment of the soul from its creator's original joy.

I was buffeted, hit, slapped with all of theses weapons and often all at the same time. The only thing that I had to defend myself was the word of God that was inside me. It was a long and painful journey, but God delivered me. He has also taught me how to remain in my state of deliverance. I want to share them with you so that satan does not get an advantage over you after God has brought you out.

Here are five (5) steps to help to stay clean after you have been delivered:

1. Remember Accountability

   (Heb.13:7, 17, 1 Thess. 5:12)

   Find a brother or sister (preferrably a Christian Leader) to watch over your life. The Bible says that two is better than one and to confess our faults one to the other.

2. Don't forsake Bible Class

   All saints oppressed or not, need to regularly draw life from the word of God.

   (2 Tim. 2:15) (Ps. 1:1-3, 119:9, 11,105,165)

3. Be humble and submissive.

    "Submit yourselves therefore to God. Resist the devil, and he will flee from you." James 4:7.

    If you resist the devil, you will be more able to submit your life to God and vice versa.

4. Get positive Fellowship - Heb. 10:24, 25.

    Find a group of saints that will accept you for who you are. Hang around people and go places where you are celebrated and not just tolerated.

5. Confess and forsake Sin as soon as you realized that it is a part of your life. (Isa. 59:2, 1 John 1:9).

Double Perfection

Along with the list of "Weapons of Death" there have been seven (7) men in my life who have had a tremendous impact either severely negative or extremely positive with a divine purpose. The males are all a type of guardian or a spiritual covering. Before God healed my heart and opened my eyes to the divine truth of the fact that with Him I have never been truly "fatherless", I felt that I hadn't had a steady covering since my grandfather (Harris) died. It was my contention that the enemy had, down through the years, somehow managed to keep this from me. There have also been a

65

number of women who have greatly impacted my life. A couple of them have been used of God to bless me, while others have been Penninah's in my life. With the exception of my mother and grandmothers, the number of women is roughly seven (7) also.

My publisher pleaded with me not to include their names in the book, and I decided to follow his advice as this book is not intended to hurt anyone. While I was in a church service one night, I was snubbed severely by one of the people who is supposed to be my "kin" by marriage. While sitting in front of me in a seat that they thought I wanted, the person turned and looked at me as if to say, "in your face". It was like they were making fun of me. I held my peace, but my Holy Ghost indignation rose up. It was as if I was in the spirit realm while the service was going on and the Lord began to show me all of the men and women who have brought joy and pain to my life. These people don't know this, but God knows it all. Some people say that seven is God's perfect number. If this is true, then 7 + 7 equals 14 which is double perfection. Could God have been using theses two sets of seven people to make me perfect (complete) or whole in His sight? I think so and I thank Him for all that He has brought me through.

"In order for you to understand my breakthrough, I had to become transparent enough to share the good,

bad and the ugly."

Annette Dunlap

<u>*Chapter VI*</u>

You Don't Know Like I Know

ca *You Don't Know Like I Know* 8ි

My habits increased with age. I was up to two packs of cigarettes a day. Marijuana became boring by itself, so I would lace it with cocaine. Sometimes now I testify in church about how I used to be on drugs and when I do, the saints probably think I just had a mild case or a light experience. To this day, even most of my family and friends don't know the full extent of my experiences with drugs and the world. I became a party animal. You could say that I was as deep into the world as a person could go. I went from cigarettes to marijuana to cocaine to hash, from hash oil to opium to poppers (inhalants) to speed (amphetamines) to acid. Acid was my favorite. I became dependent upon these drugs. I never wanted anyone to know, but I was in serious trouble. I didn't feel normal unless I had drugs in my system. Without it, I had to deal with reality and I didn't want to do that. I could drink like a fish. We would drink Remy Martin (cognac) straight and chase it with Champagne. There were times when I would hallucinate so bad, it seemed real. My weekly schedule was party, party, party. When I went to work, I would work hard so that I could make extra money so that I would be able to party even more. Sunday morning, however, I would do my best to sit back in church. Unfortunately, instead of "standing on the promises", I was just "sitting on the premises".

The devil wanted to either kill me or as the scripture says, overcharge me with the cares and glares of the world. I could easily see the word of God speaking to me. The King James Version reads like this:

And take heed to yourselves, lest at any time your hearts be overcharged with surfeiting, and drunkenness, and cares of this life, and [so] that day come upon you unawares.

Luke 21:34

The BBE (Bible in Basic English) reads like this:

But give attention to yourselves, for fear that your hearts become over-full of the pleasures of food and wine, and the cares of this life, and that day may come on you suddenly, and take you as in a net:

Luke 21:34

73

Here's how the New Living Translation says it:

Watch out! Don't let me find you living in careless ease and drunkenness, and filled with the worries of this life. Don't let that day catch you unaware,

Luke 21:34

Nobody knows like I know how tight a grip the devil had on my life; but there were many occasions where it was very clear that the Lord had His hand on me, protecting me from myself and the things that I exposed myself to. On one occasion, my grandmother found me lying in the tub. Apparently, I thought I had gotten in bed. She thought I was dead. My body was ice cold. In school we had a senior picnic that I attended, but I don't remember any of it. All I knew is that I went to the picnic with a guy and all of a sudden it was the next day and I found myself at home. My grandmother, the late Sister Mary Jane Dunlap, told me to be thankful that the guy that took me was a good friend, because he could have taken advantage of me. I was concerned that he might have, so I went to the doctor and explained that I went overboard and needed to be tested. Fortunately, they told me that everything was fine. I may have been backslidden, but who can deny that God was with me? I've been in the middle of shoot outs and other gang related activity. There were times when I would hallucinate so bad, it seemed real. One time I was at a concert, and my sister and friends

74

found me on the bathroom floor. I was in the world and in deep. The Lord had been dealing with me to come back home, but the world has a way of calling you and the flesh has a way of answering the call. I had reached a point where I was getting tired of this life. I felt like there was no reason to live, NONE! At one point in my life, I tried to commit suicide. I didn't want to live anymore. So, I took about 12 sleeping pills. For some reason my cousin, of all the times, saw me and asked me what was wrong. I told her I didn't want to live. She asked me, "What did you do?" I told her and she called my doctor and pastor.

It is funny how God operates sometimes. I tried to kill myself and he had my cousin there to stop me. I wanted Him to deliver me, take me out of the world and eventually he did, but not until he allowed me to get so full of it that I was sick of it. A friend of mine who is a pastor tells the story of when he was a child, he complained to his mother that he was so hungry that he couldn't wait for dinner. His mother assured him that dinner would be served very soon. Despite his mother's instruction and warning, he waited until she wasn't looking and took some peanut butter from the cupboard and ate it. When his father came home and discovered that he had disobeyed by eating the peanut butter, the father gave the child more of what he, the boy, claimed that he wanted. For the next full week, the child was ordered to eat peanut butter. He ate peanut butter for breakfast, peanut butter for lunch, and peanut butter for dinner. After a week of the creamy brown treat, the child never wanted to see peanut butter again. This reminds me of what God did to me. He allowed me to feed on carnality until it made me sick. I was sick of the world. Everything was happening to me. It was hell at home, no peace within and drama at church. I was catching it from all angles.

If you can give your son or daughter only one gift,

let it be enthusiasm.

Bruce Barton

<u>Chapter VII</u>

God in the House!

❧ *God in the House!* ❧

I tried to quit drugs and alcohol on my own, but I didn't have the power to do it. I would get way too sick. The withdrawals were killing me. My system was messed up. I would lock myself in my room and hurt. The pain was back. I would pray, "God help me. I don't want to die like this." I just kept praying. To ease the pain, I would get another little fix. I just couldn't stop drinking and doing drugs. I was hooked, but I prayed anyway. Whoever said that God doesn't hear a sinner's prayer was wrong! I was sinning and praying and God was listening and delivering me all the time.

One night I was sitting in the club doing my usual thing. This particular night was strange because no matter how I tried, I couldn't get high or drunk. I sat at the table drinking and smoking a cigarette. The music was right, the club was jumping, my friends were on the dance floor and I was observing the crowd. Suddenly, right in the middle of what should have been a good time, I was shut off from everyone and a voice said: "What more do I have to do?" I responded: "I don't want to be here," then it left. I wasn't frightened, I knew exactly what happened. God had stepped into the club, walked right past security, identified Himself to me, and was asking me to dance. After that, I started going back to church more and hanging out with the saints.

The more I went to church, the more I wanted to come home. In my heart, I was really ready, but I knew that I still had this problem. I didn't know how to come back to the Lord and I didn't know how I was going to kick the habit. In spite of how some of the saints treated me, I knew that God loved me and wanted me back with Him.

On December 22, 1984, there was a sister from Chicago, Illinois that came to me during altar call at a night service. She knew I was backslidden and wanted me to go to the altar. I told her that I would go for prayer, but I didn't want to come back that particular day. This was the holiday season. We had already reserved the hotel room for the parties, all the liquor had been purchased, the band was booked, and everything was set. In my heart, I wanted to come back right then and there. My flesh wanted to party one more time. So I went down for prayer. She never said a word. They began to pray for me and the next thing

I knew, God had taken over. I was speaking in tongues and couldn't stop. God had me there until He was ready for me to get up. I could hear the saints rejoicing and coaching me on. When I got up, I was completely delivered. I had no desire for cigarettes, marijuana, cocaine or alcohol. None of that stuff. God had taken it all away. I didn't have to do anything. God did it all. No AA (Alcohol Anonymous), no drug rehabilitation, just praise & worship. That part was over, but I still had to deal with the reality of not having my father.

Any saint can fall and make mistakes. God will not be as quick to judge us as we judge each other. He promises to stay married to the backslider. *Turn, O backsliding children, saith the LORD; for I am married unto you ...* (Jere. 3:14, KJV). God will not divorce His backslidden children, even when His children divorce Him.

After losing the baby, the doctors said I would never have kids because of the endometriosis that I had. As could be expected, the whole thing was a powder keg that exploded right in the middle of the church. Ironically, and in spite of the fear and drama that was brought about, the affair went on, we were attached. I was in love. For him, it was sex. Years went by and finally, I came to a breaking point, but not without a very disappointing and eye-opening experience with the men who were supposed to be there to help me.

I used to pray,
'God help me. I don't want to die like this.' They
say God doesn't hear a sinner's prayer, but I
prayed anyway, and God heard me.

Annette Dunlap

Chapter VIII

The Sins of My Fathers

❧ *The Sins of My Fathers* ❧

What do you do when you've been wounded by your spiritual fathers? Can you imagine how it feels to be gossiped about by your spiritual fathers? Can you imagine how it feels to be blackballed by your spiritual fathers, the ones that say they are watching over your souls, the ones that the Bible says are responsible for your souls? What gave them the right to stab me in my heart? Why was I considered rebellious because I didn't submit to their carnal ways? Did their position give them the right to call me a witch? Shouldn't I have refused to take the blame for something I didn't do? What happens if I confide in them and it's used against me? Why should I confess my sins and ask for forgiveness if it's going to be used against me? Why did they never take the blame for the wrongs that they did? Why do they teach that we're accountable for what we do to others, but they are not? How can I submit to whom I do not trust?

If we confess our sins, he is faithful and just to forgive us our
sins, and to cleanse us from all unrighteousness.

1 John 1:9

The book of 1 John makes it sound so simple, so promising. The way I interpreted this scripture was simple. If I would just confess my sin, God would do the rest. I could be free, free from sin, out of bondage, right with God! Apparently, those that had rule over me interpreted this scripture a whole lot differently than I did.

Everybody knows that it's our custom to visit with other churches in our religious circles. Once while we were visiting one of our sister churches, I was in the worship service. Even though the spirit was high, I thought I was going to have a nervous breakdown, and I was. It was during the altar call when the guest speaker came to me and asked me what was wrong. At first, I wouldn't say anything. Then, I spoke up and told him that I was having an affair and I wanted to confess my sins and get right with God. After I said that, I knew I was in deep. He told me that he couldn't take my confession because he was not in our council. He then referred me to one of our own district elders. This caused matters to escalate even further. I was then told that I would have to go before the diocesan because of the position my lover was in. I didn't want to do all that. I didn't want him to be in that kind of trouble. I was only concerned about me. I was confessing so I could be free of all this. I was afraid and sorry that it had all blown up the way it had, but there was always a small thought inside me that gave them the benefit of the doubt. They would handle this in a biblical way, right? They are men of God, right? They would never let me down; in fact, they should be happy that a sinner (like me) was willing to confess and admit her sin. These are my spiritual fathers and fathers are concerned about their children. Spiritual fathers are even more so concerned about the children of God. Actually, everything should have been okay because the Bible says that even heaven rejoices when a sinner comes home.

I say unto you, that likewise joy shall be in heaven over one sinner that repenteth, more than over ninety and nine just persons, which need no repentance.

Luke 15:7

I was told by one elder that I only had to talk with the diocesan, but when the time came, it seemed like the entire board was in the room. I felt like I had been lied to. I said to him, "You said it would only be me and the diocesan". He said, "Shhhhh, everything will be okay". Well it wasn't ok. First off, at the time of the meeting, I was in a backslidden state. One of the pastors said that they should not believe me because I wasn't saved. He said that I was a whore. Others agreed and called me a liar. I was so mad that I could have fought the one that called me a whore. I had to pray hard for God's forgiveness. What I felt at that time was not godly. A few months later however he died. I'm not saying he died because of how he treated me, but God knew that he was wrong for what he said to me!

As far as I was concerned, I had been betrayed. I did what the Bible said to do: I obeyed them that had the rule over me, but when I confessed my sin, my confession was used against me. The other guilty party denied everything. His wife and I fought. Not just verbally, but physically. It was horrible. When I went back home to the church, it seemed like all hell had broken loose. The saints said, "Why don't you just leave?" Some said, "Why you?" Others rolled their eyes. These people were really mad at me.

I bore the whole burden of that affair. I thought that I had done the right thing. That's all I knew to do, confess my sins, at least that's what they taught me. Later, I found out that there was one other pastor that did not like this person that I had the affair with. It was as if they tried to use the affair against him. I guess in a sense, we were both victims. As time went on, he prospered. It seemed like everyone forgot what he did and only remembered that I had accused him. I couldn't understand it. I guess in the eyes of the people, he must have been innocent. The way they treated him could not be compared to the hell that I had to endure. It almost makes you think that it is best not to even confess your sin. He denied it all and was lifted up and I confessed and was cast down. I felt like this was an injustice. So now, the wound was deeper. His wife and I had many battles. We would go to the office and talk. I remember once telling her, "I've apologized to you once and I'll say it again, I'm sorry". I remember one time she told me she forgave me, but somehow you know when a person is being disingenuous. Who could even expect her to be able to forgive me anyway? There was one time that she tried to hug me and I told her no, no, no! I didn't allow it because I felt that it wasn't real. Not long after that, we got into another fight! A few more years went by and I had a child out of wedlock from a different relationship. I wonder if church people know how cruel their words can be? When I brought the baby around, they thought they knew who the father was, but they were wrong. We would go out of town to church meetings and someone would walk up and say, "Isn't that Terrell's son?" This was just cruel. In spite of all of this, I was determined that nobody was going to run me away from the church. As time went by, things started to get better. The Lord really began to bless me. I started to regain my confidence and to feel like holding my head up.

Let all bitterness, and wrath, and anger, and clamor, and evil speaking, be put away from you, with all malice: And be ye kind one to another, tenderhearted, forgiving one another, even as God for Christ's sake hath forgiven you.

Ephesians 4:31, 32

When you are through changing,
you are through.

Author unknown

Chapter IX

The Journey

‽ *The Journey* ‽

God has always dealt with me in dreams and visions. There are probably a few spiritual gifts that He is still waiting to use me in. Many times God has taken me through a situation or an event in the spirit to prepare me for it. It is as if He takes me on small individual journeys the way He did Isaiah or John on the isle of Patmos or even Ezekiel. Now, I am certainly not comparing myself to them, but I know that God has a way of taking us to places in the spirit so that He can deal with us. One example is the time …

I danced in the spirit.

Somewhere between Monday, September 26, 2005 and Friday, October 7th, I had a vision that I was dancing in the spirit. My reaction was, "Wow, what was that all about"?
I regret that I didn't notate it right then, as I usually do, however, I was rejoicing about something.

Everybody should seek God for a revelation of His mind and will, but take my advice, don't worry about what He is saying when He speaks to you. Just wait, God will always make His word clear. Where there is a journey, a vision or a promise, you can always be sure that there will be ...

A Manifestation

Sunday, October 9th, 2005, I went to my home church. They were having their October Fest. They also had a highly anointed speaker that day. The power of God came in so strong, it was like I couldn't contain myself. It started in a worship environment and then it changed to praise. I know this sounds backward to some, but this is how it happened. I was dancing and dancing and dancing. The power of God was on me real strong. It didn't hit me until Tuesday, October 11th, 2005, that I had already danced in the spirit.

Pastors, prominent ministers, sociologists and others have for years debated and discussed the role of the black church. If you are not an apostolic saint of God, you are probably wondering why so much of my life and emotion is centered on the people that I went to church with. Part of the answer is obvious. The trials and experiences that I had to endure were brought about by the church and church people. Did I bring some

99

of it on myself? Of course I did, but look at the church a little differently than most people. When a person goes to a hospital emergency room, the hospital staff looks beyond the faults of the injured and simply scrambles to their rescue and tries to save their life. When will the church learn its true role? When will the people of God finally understand that the church is a hospital, not a place for finger pointing? Why are we so amazed to see the sick and wounded among us? Why is the church among the few institutions that kills its wounded? With all of its problems, we who are members of it know very well that for us the black church is a strong time honored institution. It is a house of prayer for those who need a corporate connection. It is a house of refuge for those who have been in trouble. It is a hospital for those who are new converts and unknown to the local congregation. The church is also just plain old "home" to a great number of us. That's why I refer to my experiences as I moved from one assembly to another as a "journey". Any time you leave home, it's a journey, especially if for a while you are considered homeless. After being dealt with so dramatically and directly by God, I returned to my church home. I didn't know what to expect, but things started off pretty slow. After a while I started to feel like I would be okay. It took me some time to get back into the flow of things, and I noticed that little by little the saints' anger seemed to cool. I remember thinking, "Now I've got to just stay cautious". I didn't want to be hurt and I certainly didn't want to mess up my new standing. No matter how cautious I was, some people just couldn't help but be themselves and try to keep a little drama going. When new members came in, I was referred to as "the one that had the affair". Some wives would even caution other wives to look out for me, because I would try to take their man. Never mind that we believed in God's total redemption. Never mind that I was accepted back into the fold publicly. Never mind that they heard me speak in tongues and you can absolutely forget anything that the Bible says. The saints would make sure that newcomers were informed of my past, but in reality, what should I have expected? Although, these are church people, they are still patients in the hospital. As time went on, things started to get better. I was working very diligently in the music department, served as youth leader; I was called to preach and had other functions in this ministry. Then, I started to get bored with it all. I knew there was more to God than this and I wanted it. The Lord began to deal with me about leaving. I could hardly believe it. Why would God want or even allow me to leave? I said to myself, "But this is my home". My family was there. I grew up there. I had all kinds of excuses. I could not imagine leaving my home. Besides, I didn't know where I was going. I needed a scripture and the Lord started dealing with me about Abraham. He told Abraham to leave his kindred, so I began to feel a little better. I gradually started to back out of all my positions.

I was seeking God day in and day out about where He wanted me to go. Then, I had a vision. I was in a building and my ex-husband was there. There were a few more people there too and I believe there were two policemen (authority figures). I left the building and ran into a huge field. The field was filled with trees. I was running and my ex-husband was running behind me. Then he dropped off the scene and I kept running. I turned around and saw myself getting further away so I started running back to the building. Then, I heard a voice that said, "Spare the small steps." When I got back to the building, it was empty. No one was there. I still didn't know what to do or where to go. I asked a pastor about the words and He said whatever God is telling you to do, He wants you to take a big, giant step and just do it. Somehow, I knew he was right. I was then convinced that it was time to go, but go where? I didn't have a clue. God began to deal with me about Joshua. He began to deal with me about crossing over Jordan, going to the other side. I went to a convention and the speaker was saying the same thing. When I got back home, the following Sunday, I told my mother I was going to visit a church and I'll be back. When I got there, he was preaching the very same text. He had started a chapter by chapter series. Then I went the following Sunday and then to Bible Class. I knew this wasn't coincidental. I went again one Sunday and during the message, my spirit leaped. I felt like Elizabeth when John the Baptist leaped inside her. I knew then, that it was confirmed. I had a hard time. I struggled because I loved the youth choir at my home church. I told God that I couldn't leave my kids. He reminded me that they were His. I had another vision. We were at church and the choir was on the 3rd floor. As I was walking across the parking lot, some of the choir members were outside. I asked them why they were not inside, nobody responded. We all went in. I had the boom-box in my hand. When we got to the 3rd floor, there were some older church members up there. We began to start rehearsing, "The Lord Is Blessing Me Right Now." I told one of the other girls to turn off the CD. She couldn't. I told her again, and she really couldn't. It was really frustrating because the choir would not obey me and that's not like them. So, I went over to turn off the CD myself. It would not turn off. It was like it was stuck on the vamp of, "The Lord Is Blessing me." That's all that kept playing. Then we got in line and went downstairs to go into the sanctuary. I went down the hall and the scene changed. I still had on my Sunday dress but it was another scene. I was at my home. When I opened the door to go into the sanctuary, there were the steps at my grandmother's house - my home; I put my head in my hands and told the Lord, "Okay". I said, "Yes". It was time to go. I thought it was very striking that I was 40 years old when I left. I went and talked with my pastor and left with his blessings. The really crazy thing is that when I got there, the first lady made mention about me being there for a season. That's the one thing I really do appreciate about them. They really understand time and season. After being there a few months, I knew why I was there. I was there to be purged. Oh, my gosh, I was so hurt with what was revealed about me inwardly. I had taken on the ugliness of religious formalism. I didn't realize how ugly being religious really was. I didn't know how ugly traditionalism really was. I couldn't see that we were putting our noses up and looking down on people if they didn't look like what we were taught. After church, I would go to my car and cry. I repented so much, that God probably said, "OK, OK, OK, OK". This was a very intense time for me. Soon, it was time to move again. The Lord allowed just the right amount of drama which let me know that it was time to go. I felt like, I had been cleansed. I knew that I had, but there was one more thing. I had held a grudge against a sister at this assembly for two years. The pastor was doing a series on attitudes. This particular week, he talked about the heart and challenged us to get things right with each other. I realized that he was right and I talked with the sister, apologized and repented. With that, I thought that everything was done and over. WRONG! The apology took place on a Sunday. Thursday of that week, I was called on into a meeting in the pastor's office and questioned about this and some other things that I was accused of. Now, I'm the kind of person that when and if there's a problem, I believe in calling all parties involved, working it out, but that was not the custom at this church. They took the other person's word for it and then they sat me down and left me down. I didn't put up an argument. Did it hurt? Yes! But for some reason, it was okay. I was getting too comfortable there anyway. Looking back on it now, I think it had to happen for me to leave. That confession thing was not working out for me. The pastor there was not interested in making the situation right and it was time for me to go. The next assembly I went to was smaller than the one I left. I didn't understand. I went from a large established assembly to a small assembly. There was a lot of work to be done there. The one thing I did like about this assembly was that, the people were real. They didn't come up in church. They were straight from the street. In that, I watched how God cleaned up some of these people during my time there. It made sense. If I had left my original church and came straight to this one, I would not have been able to take it. It was a work canvassing, helping them to build and maintain what they had. However, sometimes help can be read the wrong way. I could deal with that, but the betrayal was too much for me to handle. One day I was reaching for something on the back seat of my car and my Bible was open. I grabbed it and read the passage where it was opened. I said to myself, "Oh Lord, you don't really mean that!!" I could not shake this scripture. I left exactly how the passage described. God always has a plan. We have to follow it to get to our destiny. The church where I fellowship now is smaller than the last one. I know you may say what does that have to do with anything? It doesn't. I just didn't understand it at that particular time. God wants me to long for Him, not the size of the church. Maybe that's why He's put me where I am now. There has been a lot of healing throughout this journey. Enough healing that I can now sit and write about it in order to help someone else.

Some people love you because you are smart, helpful, beautiful or rich. Sometimes they admire your personality, your dimples, or the way you wear your hair. Some people are infatuated with your charms others with your verbosity. Even parents have an emotional and psychological attachment to their children that result in love. God loves you also, but not because of you. God is not moved by your physical attributes and qualities. He loves you simply because he chooses to. His love is self-generated, unmotivated, and never ending.

L. McNeese

<u>Chapter X</u>

Lord, You're Kidding, Right?

Lord, You're Kidding, Right?

ᗿ *Lord, You're Kidding, Right?* ᔥ

Leaving the church was a bittersweet journey that ultimately proved to be God's way of getting me free from some remaining emotional and spiritual strongholds. Leaving however didn't get me off the hook totally. About two years ago, I was sitting at my desk at work. I felt in my spirit that the Holy Ghost was telling me to go to Terrell's wife and apologize to her again. I said, "You're kidding. Why, I've already done that?" Oh, I was so outdone. I waited a couple of more days and it got stronger. I called a dear friend of mine and told her about it. She said, "Go, if you want me to, I'll go with you." I told her she didn't have to, but that I would go. So, I called and asked, "Can you meet me? I need to talk with you." At first she said, "No". She wouldn't have time today. I gave her my number so that she could call me when it was convenient. She called right back and said she would. I told the Lord if this is really Him, He would

110

have to make provisions. I had to pick up my son and I didn't have a baby sitter. I called my aunt and she kept him for me. I went to the location and she wasn't there. I thought, good, maybe it wasn't God. Maybe it was me. I was about to leave when I looked around and saw her approaching. I felt like asking, "God, please don't make me do this." It was killing me. We met at the church and when we began to talk, I figured that she had a small tape recorder or someone was around listening. It didn't matter. I told her that I felt the presence of God telling me to come and apologize again. I told her that I was so sorry for hurting her and I asked her to forgive me. God knows this was one of the hardest things I've ever had to do. She stood up and looked me in the face and said, "Yes, I forgive you." This was a release. Yes! She began to minister to me for the first time in our tainted history. It felt like tons of weights were lifted off me. She told me that she has hurt people also and has had to ask for forgiveness. We began to rejoice. I had to break out in a dance. There was no music, just us. Oh, I felt so much lighter. As I was leaving, she said, "I love you." I cried the rest of the day. It was such an overwhelming day. So far, she has treated me with nothing but kindness. There was a time that I could never imagine her and me joking and laughing together.

<u>*Chapter XI*</u>

The Death of Temptation

.

ଔ*The Death of Temptation* ଵ

*The Lord knows how to deliver the godly out of temptation
and to keep the unrighteous under punishment for
the day of judgment.*

II Peter 2:9

Not long after that the repaired relationship, I had a vision. I was at my former church. I was praying and it seemed like I was caught up in the spirit (or in some kind of trance). Suddenly, I saw Terrell in a casket. The pews were mats and it seemed like people were not sitting, but instead were all lying down. Terrell was in the casket on his back and then turned over. It appeared as if he was praying. He got out of the casket and started walking up the right side of the church, waving goodbye. He came up the aisle and went out the door, when he came back in, he was in the row that my sister and I were on. I was lying next to my sister. I was so shaken that I put my head under the covers because I didn't want to see him. While under the covers I

114

heard something shut. I thought that he had gotten back in the casket and closed it. I peeked out from under the covers and he was at my feet. He said, "Bye" and waved. I said, "Bye", and then he got back in the casket and I woke up.

When I woke up, the interest that I had in him had gone out of me. I've never looked at him the same since. Since then, when I tried to share this with men who are pastors and were supposed to be friends of mine, they would always seem to turn their backs on me with the exception of two.

I have always been amazed and disappointed that I had to be openly put to shame and bear all of the burden for what happened by myself. Terrell came to me secretly and made a one-on-one apology, but never an open apology. To this day, he has allowed me to look like I lied about our affair. In the eyes of the saints, he's innocent. But that's okay. As it stands today, not only did I get over him, God DELIVERED me from him. The grip of temptation that satan had on me died. God placed it in that coffin and buried it in a sea of forgetfulness. It is amazing to think about how I was so into him at one time and he was so into me, but God took that spirit right out of me. I can honestly say that I am totally healed and free from that part of my life. I pray to God that he would also repent if he hasn't. If you look at him today, he looks troubled, like something is heavy on his mind, and according to Isaiah 57:21, "There is no peace ...," says my God, "for the wicked."

<u>Chapter XII</u>

I Had to Fight For It

CR*I Had To Fight For It* SO

I believe that our lives are foreordained by God. I also believe that we have an expected end according to Jeremiah 29:11.

> *For I know the thoughts that I think toward you, saith the Lord, thoughts of peace, and not of evil, to give you an expected end.*

However, that does not mean there won't be a fight. I think we all know that. The Bible tells us that faith without works is dead. When I decided to live, I knew I had to fight. I've always been a fighter. I just had misplaced anger, but I refused to let the enemy have any more control over my life and I refused to let the enemy have my promise. At one point, I was just sitting by allowing the devil to take everything from me. No more, I began to face reality and fight for my life, my destiny. I had to first fight for my own sanity. I began to face my pain, issues and enemies. I learned to fight in the spirit realm.

For the weapons of our warfare are not carnal, but mighty through God to the pulling down of strong holds; Casting down imaginations, and every high thing that exalteth itself against the knowledge of God, and bringing into captivity every thought to the obedience of Christ;

II Corinthians 10:4-5

Since then, my prayer life has increased. I began to pray and meditate constantly. I got in my word like never before. It had to work for me. The word of the Lord was my only hope. I had gotten to a point where I knew God was calling me to consecrate myself in fasting and prayer because He wanted to speak to me.

(The Vision)

On Sunday, August 22, 2004, somewhere between 6:30-7:45a.m., I had a vision. I was at a church service and some of my former church members were there. Actually, the church was very similar to my home church. It was as if I had gone back to this assembly. I was talking to a couple of sisters who were actually blood sisters. They were asking me about my son. I told them that he was still at our former church. One of the sisters told me that I should have made him come with me. I told her that the Lord has always taken care of us in our moves. I later moved down closer to the front of the church. The pastor's wife was sitting on the right hand side of the church, closer to the front. Then, the seating changed in the church. There were pews facing the pulpit where the rhythm section would be. I saw my grandfather, the late District Elder W.W. Harris. He was smiling. He had the guest speaker by the arm like he was trying to show him someone. I knew daddy was looking for me. I was sitting on the end of the seat. I partly stood up and started to wave, signaling my granddaddy where I was. He saw me and came over. He brought the speaker with him. The speaker had on a white robe. He told the speaker, "Here she is!" Daddy spoke to me and left. The speaker smiled and said, "I have a word for you from the Lord concerning him." I said, "Him?" He looked at me and said, "Him". He said it as if to say, you know exactly who I'm talking about. He said, "I'm not going to lay hands on you or none of that. I'm just going to tell you and you better get on your knees, bow down, lift your hands or do something". Then the speaker went away. I got on my knees and told the Lord, "Thank you!", then I had to wait. (That was the hard part.)

(The Word of the Lord Came)

On Sunday, November 28, 2004, the Lord woke me up about 6:30 a.m. A sister at the church appeared to me. She had on a red dress and her hair was in an updo. She looked like she was dressed for Sunday morning service. She was standing as if she was in testimony service. She said, "Luke 13:12". She didn't quote it, she just said numerical portions of the scripture. I immediately jumped up and got my Bible. The scripture said,

"And when Jesus saw her, he called her to him, and said unto her, "Woman, thou art loosed from thine infirmity"."

At first, I didn't get it. Then it dawned on me. That was the word. That's why the speaker that appeared to me told me to say, "thank you". The next verse, 13 says,

"And he laid hands on her: and immediately she was made straight and glorified God."

I was waiting on the laying of hands part. Then it dawned on me again. I was told that there would be no laying of hands. It was just the spoken word. I had thanked God in advance. I have to be honest. Even after that, I was still a little puzzled. Initially, I thought the Lord loosed me from a guy I had been dating. I was on an emotional roller coaster ride with him. This wasn't the case, but it helped. I was loosed from that spirit that had me bowed down. Now, I'm standing upright in my spirit.

In preparation for the writing of this book I sought the Lord on many occasions as to what He wanted me to say to His people. As I was riding to work one morning, it dropped in my spirit that God wants to be a personal father to some. He wants to be a father to us all, but unfortunately, everybody will not strive to have that kind of relationship with God. I know that more than ever now. Whenever this happens, God always backs it up in His Word. He said, "It's like Jesus", meaning that Joseph was his earthly father, but Jesus knew his real dad. When Mary and Joseph wanted to know where he was, the reply was, "I'm about my father's business, I'm doing the work of my Father." My question to you is, "Will you be made whole? Will you allow God to be the father that you never knew?

The forces of evil might have the ability to frighten us, hinder us and cause us to experience undo stress. However, we have authority over everything that he is able to do.

Dr. Johnny Burrell

<u>*Chapter XIII*</u>

Imagine

ᗋ*Imagine* ᔆ

I magine you're my father standing tall above the crowd, the mighty under-shepherd, looking good and talking loud. Imagine I'm your child and your wish is my command. My spiritual existence and my soul is in your hands. Imagine that I trusted you and in a private session I tried to make it right with God by leaving my confessions. Imagine it is a perfect world where all things go your way and people feel, think, and do the things that you say. Now imagine that I'm in trouble and I am coming to you in pain expecting you to do the job that Jesus Christ ordained. You teach that we're held accountable for everything we do, but it seems that the word of God is binding everyone, but you. Is it my imagination that you never take the blame when your and my transgressions are inherently the same? Is it real or am I dreaming when my private words to you are spread across the sacred desk and used to make me blue? Did I disrupt your perfect world where no one has a fault where you abuse me as you wish and think you won't be caught? You never say that you're sorry and you make my life so hard, and if I leave your carnal house you say that I left the Lord. My God is in the heavens and He knows my heart is true. He also knows that I hold you up in prayer the way a saint should do. And when we all ascend on high to answer for our work, imagine how you're going to feel to see the hearts you've hurt.

Always remember that God has designed your purpose in life and in ministry; seek to do His will.

Dr. Marc Edgar Royster, Sr.

<u>Chapter XIV</u>

The Final Analysis

❧ *The Final Analysis* ❧
- *Counting my Blessings* -

In 1897 song writer Johnson Oatman penned the words to a song that I think every saint should believe, read and obey. God has blessed each and every one of us in so many different ways that it is really unnecessary to sit around and allow bitterness to build up in us. Life is full of troubles, but it is also full of blessings. Listen to Johnson Oatman:

When upon life's billows
You are tempest tossed
When you are discouraged
Thinking all is lost
Count your many blessings
Name them one by one
And it will surprise you
What the Lord has done.

134

Count your blessings
Name them one by one
Count your blessings
See what God has done
Count your blessings
Name them one by one
Count your many blessings
See what God has done.

Are you ever burdened
With a load of care? Does
the cross seem heavy You
are called to bear? Count
your many blessings Every
doubt will fly
And you will be singing
As the days go by.

Count your blessings
Name them one by one
Count your blessings
See what God has done
Count your blessings
Name them one by one
Count your many blessings
See what God has done

When you look at others
With their lands and gold
Think that Christ has promised
You His wealth untold
Count your many blessings
Money cannot buy Your
reward in heaven Nor
your home on high.

So, amid the conflict
Whether great or small
Do not be discouraged
God is over all
Count your many blessings
Angels will attend Help
and comfort give you To
your journey's end.

Count your blessings
Name them one by one
Count your blessings
See what God has done
Count your blessings
Name them one by one
Count your many blessings. See what God has done.

When I look back over my life, and I think things over I can truly say that I am blessed. Regardless of what has happened to me, God has been there all the time.

- I made peace with Terrell's wife.
- After the doctors said that I would never have kids I had a beautiful baby boy.
- I was called to preach after all that I had both done and been through.
- I have a healthy and satisfying relationship with my biological father.
- I am happy.

- God spared my life from suicide.

- God kept me from being the victim of a date rape.

- God delivered me from inappropriate feelings.

- I am delivered from drugs.

- I do not drink alcohol.

- I do not want either of the above.

- God delivered me from bitterness.

- God locked away my temptation in a casket.

God has made me immune from the weapons of death:

- I know that I'm not rejected and feelings of rejection do not torment me anymore.

- I know that I'm forgiven and I am able to forgive others for their trespasses.

- I realize that I don't have to lie to anyone. God has given me the strength to walk in integrity.

- A man does not validate me; God has taught me how to love myself.

- God has not given me the spirit of fear and through His word I have become strong, able to stand against adversity.

- I can do all things through Christ; I don't have time for the devil.

- God has taught me how to control my anger so that it doesn't overcome me.

- Christ has forgiven me my sins and I am learning to forgive others of theirs.

"What more do I have to do?"

- God

Bibliography

Burrell, Johnny, D.D., *Hell is Not in Charge (Positive Proof that satan is a Wimp).* Kearney, NE; I.T.N.O.J. Publishing, Clarksville, TN 2005

Erickson, Millard J., *Christian Theology Second Edition.* Grand Rapids, MI; Baker Academic, 1998.

Lucado, Max, *Mocha with Max (Friendly thoughts & simple Truths from the writings of . . .).* Nashville, TN; J. Countryman, 2005

McNeese, La Monte, *The Top 10 Dumbest Christian Beliefs.* Bloomington, IN; Authorhouse Publishing, 2004

Morgan, Robert J., *Then Sings My Soul Book 2 (150 of the world's greatest hymn stories).* Nashville, TN; Thomas Nelson, Inc.; 2004

Royster, Marc Edgar, Sr., *Are You Sure God Told You to Tell Me That?* Kearney, NE; 2000

Shelton Danny & Quinn Shelley J., *Ten Commandments Twice Removed.* Remnant Publications, Inc., 2006.

The Holy Bible. Nashville, TN; Broadman & Holman Publishers, 1987

Unwin Stephen D., *The Probability of God (A simple calculation that proves the ultimate truth).* New York, NY; Crown Forum; 2003

Webster, Noah 1828, *American Dictionary of the English Language*. San Francisco, CA; Foundation of the American Christian Education; May 2002.

Webster's New World College Dictionary fourth edition. New York, NY; A Pearson Education Macmillan Company; 1999

Glossary

1. <u>Adage</u> – a proverb; an old saying

2. <u>Buffet</u> – to strike with hand or fist; to box; to beat

3. <u>Ralph Waldo Emerson</u> – a nineteenth century American lecturer and author; a leader of transcendentalism

4. <u>Culture Shock</u> - the <u>anxiety</u> and <u>feelings</u> (surprise, disorientation, confusion) felt when people have to operate within an entirely different cultural or <u>social environment</u>

5. <u>Domineering</u> – ruling with insolence, arrogant, overbearing, tyrannical, imperious

6. <u>Endometriosis</u> – a medical condition where tissue like that which lines the <u>uterus</u> is found outside the womb in other areas of the body. A major symptom of endometriosis is pain, mostly in the lower abdomen, lower back, and pelvic area. Women with this disease may have disabling mentrual cramps, pain during intercourse, bowl movements and urination.

7. <u>Envy</u> – painful or resentful awareness of another's advantage joined with the desire to possess the same advantage

8. <u>Enthusiasm</u> – intense or eager interest; zeal; fervor

9. <u>Epistles</u> – written correspondence, whether personal or official. The Old Testament abounds with evidences of widespread written letters. The term most often refers to the 21 epistles of the New Testament, written by four

maybe five writers: Peter, Paul, John, Jude and the writer of Hebrews (possibly Paul).

10. <u>Fatherless</u> – person without a male parent; not knowing who one's father is

11. <u>Love</u> – unselfish, loyal and benevolent intention and commitment toward another

12. <u>Mocha</u> – a choice kind of coffee, originally exported from Mocha, in Arabia, flavored with coffee or coffee and chocolate

13. <u>Mockery</u> – a subject of laughter or ridicule

14. <u>Peninnah</u> - one of the two wives of <u>Elkanah</u> (<u>1 Samuel 1:2-7</u>)The other wife was <u>Hannah</u>, who bore no children for many years. Peninnah apparently was mentally cruel to Hannah and "provoked her sore" about her inability to have children. After much earnest prayer and a promise to God, Hannah bore <u>Samuel</u> who became a great priest of Israel.
An arch rival, one, especially a female, who taunts or teases another causing great pain and emotional turmoil.

15. <u>PhD</u> – an abbreviation for the <u>Latin</u> "*Philosophiæ Doctor*" or alternatively "*Doctor philosophiæ*", a <u>doctoral</u> degree is granted at the completion of extensive academic work in a particular field of study. Although originally granted exclusively for work in <u>philosophy,</u> today Ph.D.s are awarded in nearly all fields of the sciences and humanities. The highest degree awarded in a field is usually a PhD.

16. <u>Post-doctoral</u> - of or relating to study or research that is done after work for the doctoral degree has been completed

17. <u>Rejected</u> – thrown away, cast off, refused, slighted

18. <u>Series of events</u>: a complicated series of events or personal experiences stretching over a considerable period of time, or a detailed account of such a series of events or experiences

19. <u>School of Hard Knocks</u> – an imaginary school whose program of study consists only of the practical knowledge imparted by life experience.

20. <u>Surfeiting</u> – to feed or supply to satiety or excess

21. <u>Variance</u> – an active disagreement; quarrel; dispute

22. <u>Wiles</u> – sly tricks, deceitful artifices, stratagems

<u>Other IPC Publications include:</u>

Are you Sure God Told you to Tell me That?
Marc Royster

Hell is Not in Charge!
Johnny Burrell

Accessing the Leader in You
Carl McCullen

Jabez, What's in a Name?
Mario V. Price

How to be Strong When Falsely Accused
L. McNeese

I Found My Mind in '79
Harvey Brown

Robbing God?
La Monte McNeese

A Parallel Guide to the Scriptures
Charlene Burnett

Jesus The Ultimate Ology
Johnny James

Rebuilding Lives Through the Spirit
Michael L. Boyd

The Greatest Quotes of the Walking Bible, Johnny James
La Monte McNeese

What God Will Do if You Let Him
Dorothy A. Miller